COPYRIGHTS/CREDITS

Little Miss Mason Jar

ISBN-13: 978-1492317760
ISBN-10: 1492317764

Edited by **Staci Mildenberger**
Photography by **Whitney Fletcher Photography** www.whitneyfletcherphotography.com

Cover Picture / Author Picture Venue by **Sweet South Cottage** www.sweetsouthcottage.com
Graphic Design by **Samantha Fielder** www.etsy.com/shop/PaperField
Cover Design & Book Formatting by **Nancy A. Brown** www.virtualgalfriday.com

Legal Notices

DEDICATION

This book is written in memory of my grandmother. She turned grilled cheese sandwiches into gold and baked chocolate chip cookies fit for a king. The fragrant food she prepared paved roads of memories in my mind that will last forever. Everyone claims their grandma was the best cook in the world.

Mine really was!

TABLE OF CONTENTS

INTRODUCTION

Cooking is a long held passion of mine. Slicing and dicing my way to a culinary creation puts a smile on my face and tasty treats on the table for my family. Despite this passion, I often find myself in the midst of dinnertime drama.

My weeknights are crammed with heavy loads of homework, piles of dirty dishes in the sink, multiple afterschool activities and a fatigued family who still desperately wants to enjoy a home cooked meal together after these busy and bustling days.

So, in an effort to simplify suppertime, I made the decision to start batch cooking each Sunday afternoon for the week. I planned and prepared meals in mason jars and tucked them away in the refrigerator or freezer for future use. Almost immediately, my mason jar obsession got out of hand and Little Miss Mason Jar was born. Little Miss Mason Jar discovered quickly how these jars were saving her suppertime sanity. I taught myself how to make lunches in mason jars to help relieve my morning rush and get me out the door more quickly.

Of course, then Little Miss Mason Jar saw more opportunities even for making breakfast, snacks and sweet treats in this fun and efficient new way. Making the transformation from stressed out wife and mother to Little Miss Mason Jar has improved my life on many levels. I can't measure the amount of joy it gives me to hit the sack each Sunday night knowing all dinner dilemmas are solved for the coming week. I can open the refrigerator to a selection of savory supper choices ready to dish up in no time. And because everything looks better in a mason jar (Believe me, you will see!), this make-ahead tactic has worked wonders for my bad habit of forgetting left-overs stashed away in the back of the refrigerator. Okay, maybe I don't actually forget they are there, maybe I choose not to eat them. Surely they are rotten and rancid after twenty-four hours of fridge time, right? Wrong!

Being able to see the fresh food jam-packed inside of the jars helps me clean out the fridge by the time Friday rolls around and NOTHING goes to waste. Little Miss Mason Jar also appreciates the health benefit of storing food in glass containers instead of pesky plastic as an added perk to this method of cooking.

Most of the mason jar meals in this book are prepared or cooked directly in a mason jar. However, some recipes involve simply storing the main element of the recipe in a mason jar to facilitate faster assembly when cooking. Mason jars make such cute and convenient containers that I've even included some ideas for sippin' pretty drinks and fun ways for displaying snacks. Even mason jar lids are featured in a few recipes for baking dainty and delicious pies. They don't call me Little Miss Mason Jar for nothing!

Mason jars can endure extreme temperatures which make them conducive to cooking and baking. They make excellent individual serving pieces for personal portions and are perfect for packaging edible gifts to share with others. Take one to a teacher to show appreciation, welcome a new neighbor or send get-well-wishes to someone under the weather by making them a mason jar meal to help them heal.

This mason jar meal cookbook does not even mention canning and preserving topics typically associated with cooking with mason jars. Instead, this mason jar meal manuscript is filled with modern meals packed with personality and overflowing with flavor and fun. If you need a little encouragement in the kitchen or culinary chaos is lurking in your life, have no fear. Little Miss Mason Jar is here!

MASON JAR SIZES AND SLANG

quart — 4 cups tall pint — 2 cups short pint — 2 cups tall half-pint — 1 cup short half-pint — 1 cup mini mason jar — 1/2 cup

LITTLE MISS MASON JAR USES THESE FAMILIAR FAVORITES FOR COOKING AND BAKING

Mason jars are made in all shapes and sizes. They come in big, small, short, tall and everything in between. Some mason jars have measurement marks on them so you can keep track of the amount of food or liquid along the way and you can even use them as measuring cups. Companies that manufacture mason jars often release special edition jars so be on the lookout for new replicas to reinforce supplies.

The wide mouth jars have a large opening and are ideal for most mason jar meals. However, any mason jar will work and the sizes and shapes listed for each recipe are just suggestions of what Little Miss Mason Jar recommends. Short and wide mason jars work well too and make it easier to scoop out goodies.

There is a lot of mason jar jargon throughout this cookbook. In order to help you figure out which size or shape you will need you can use this page for reference. Buying mason jars won't break the bank, which is just one more reason to love them. Typically sold by the dozen for around ten dollars, they are very affordable. Most chain stores and even grocery stores sell mason jars in bulk. If you are in search for specialty sizes or special edition mason jars, head to your local craft store for an expansive, but more expensive selection.

LITTLE MISS MASON JAR'S
<u>MUST KNOW</u> TIPS FOR MAKING MEALS IN MASON JARS

Sterilize and/or wash every mason jar and lid before each use. They are not fun to wash, but then again, I can't think of any dish that is!

When freezing food in a mason jar, make sure you leave room at the top for expansion. Little Miss Mason Jar got carried away once and overfilled some mason jars with homemade spaghetti sauce before putting them in the freezer. One jar actually cracked open at the bottom and sauce seeped everywhere in the refrigerator while defrosting. Leave about one inch of room between the food and the rim of the jar when freezing to avoid making this same mistake. If you forget, you'll only forget once!

Wide-mouth jars are the best to use but regular jars work as well. Wide-mouth jars make it easier to fill with food and to pour out. When eating straight from the jar, the wide-mouth also comes in handy.

When placing the mason jars in the oven to cook, place them on a jelly roll pan with sides. This will help keep them stable and easy to maneuver. Removing mason jars from the oven can be daunting and dangerous. Use extreme caution and have plenty of pot holders on hand.

If you will be eating straight from your mason jar allow the jars to cool for ten to fifteen minutes before serving and remember that the jars will be hot.

An ice cream scoop works well for placing food inside mason jars. Funnels, zip top bags and pastry bags are always on-hand in my kitchen for this purpose.

Always wipe the rims when finished assembling a mason jar meal. This will keep them clean and looking cute.

When making salads in mason jars add the dressing first so it will be at the bottom of the jar and layer the ingredients with the most fragile or delicate ingredients like lettuce at the top. The ingredients will stay separated and will not get soggy if layered correctly. When you are ready to eat the salad, shake the jar to distribute the dressing. Salads should be taken out of the fridge at least thirty minutes before eating to allow the dressing to liquefy and, therefore, become perfectly shakable.

Beware, using mason jars of a size other than those suggested by Little Miss Mason Jar, may require an adjusted cooking time. Longer cooking time will be needed for larger jars and less time will be needed for smaller jars.

When planning to cook mason jar meals that have been held in the refrigerator beforehand, allow them thirty minutes to sit at room temperature before baking for best results.

For foods that are baked in mason jars, you may want to seal them right away to keep them as fresh as possible for later use. To seal, carefully use a pot holder or kitchen towel to screw the lids on the mason jars as soon as they come out of the oven. Within ten minutes you should hear a popping sound which means the mason jars have sealed. That sound is music to Little Miss Mason Jar's ears!

MASON JAR MAKEOVERS

Mason jars are charming and appealing on their own, but Little Miss Mason Jar likes to add a little fun and flair by using simple supplies to dress them up. Raid your craft closet for materials such as ribbon, trim, lace, craft tape, bakers twine, burlap, scrapbook paper, stencils, fabric and chalkboard paint.

Your pantry has plenty of useful items to makeover mason jars like coffee filters, jumbo cupcake liners and paper doilies. For an adorable edible gift, attach a wooden or plastic spoon or fork to the mason jar with twine.

Mason jar labels and chalkboard paint will perk up mason jar meals and provide a personal touch.

MASON JARS IN THE MORNING

Breakfast is not Little Miss Mason Jar's preferred meal of the day. During the work week, our mornings turn our home into a madhouse. On the weekends, slowly sipping a cup of coffee and reading the newspaper is how I spend my mornings.

(Cue Mr. Mason Jar's favorite comment, *"Breakfast is the most important part of the day".*)

I do realize that eating breakfast is salient to starting the day properly, so I created mason jar breakfast meals to bring more mellow to our mornings.

With mason jars in the morning I can rise and shine with ease and eat breakfast as I please.

BANANA BREAD

Little Miss Mason Jar doesn't monkey around when it comes to banana bread. This recipe uses whole-wheat flour and the toasted walnuts could easily be traded out for one cup of dark chocolate chips. To reheat them in the morning (or anytime), remove the top of the mason jar and microwave for twenty to thirty seconds. The bread will slide right out or serve them with a fork and enjoy them straight from the jar. These make adorable hostess gifts or teacher treats. Trust Little Miss Mason Jar, everyone will go 'bananas' for these!

Ingredients

1 cup sugar
1 stick butter, softened
2 eggs
3 large very ripe bananas
½ cup buttermilk
1 teaspoon vanilla
1 teaspoon cinnamon
1½ cups all-purpose flour
1 cup whole wheat flour
1 teaspoon baking soda
1 teaspoon salt
¼ cup premade cinnamon-sugar mixture
Cooking spray
1 cup walnuts, toasted (optional)

Directions

1. Preheat oven to 325 degrees. Grease ten tall half-pint jars with cooking spray. Sprinkle one teaspoon of cinnamon-sugar inside the jar to coat the bottom and sides (optional).

2. In a large bowl, stir sugar and butter together until smooth. Add eggs and mix well. Stir in bananas, buttermilk, vanilla and cinnamon with a spoon until combined. Stir in flours, baking soda and salt until just moistened. Stir in nuts or chocolate chips – or some of both!

3. Fill jars half way and place carefully in oven for thirty minutes.

4. Remove from oven carefully and immediately screw on the lids and listen for them to seal within ten minutes. Let cool.

MINI CINI ROLLS

The smell of cinnamon rolls baking in the oven on a Saturday morning provides a sweet wakeup call to start your family's weekend off right. Bake up a batch of these cute creations on the weekend and stick any leftovers in the refrigerator. If there are any left come Monday morning, remove the mason jar lids and reheat them in the microwave for twenty to thirty seconds and begin your week with a homemade mini cini.

You can make these two ways – using a mini mason jar (4-ounce) or a short half-pint mason jar. It depends on how mini you want your cini!

<u>Ingredients</u>

1 8-count tube refrigerated Crescent Rolls
4 tablespoons softened butter
½ cup brown sugar
1 tablespoon cinnamon

To prepare the icing, mix the following ingredients in a bowl using a whisk

1 cup powdered sugar
2 tablespoons milk
1 teaspoon vanilla
1 tablespoon premade cinnamon-sugar mix

Directions

1. Roll out the crescent rolls on a cutting board and flatten into a rectangle, pressing seams together.
2. Combine softened butter, brown sugar and cinnamon. Spread over the entire crescent roll rectangle.
3. Roll up the crescent roll, jelly roll style.

For four ounce mini mason jars, cut two inch slices of the crescent roll and place one slice in each mini mason jar. Carefully place jars in the oven and cook at 350 degrees for fifteen minutes. Remove jars from oven and let cool two to three minutes before drizzling icing on top.

For half-pint mason jars, cut one inch slices of the crescent rolls and place four pieces together, touching, in the mason jars. Carefully place jars in the oven and cook at 350 degrees for eighteen to twenty minutes. Remove jars from oven and let cool two to three minutes before drizzling icing on top.

SOUTHERN GRITS CAKES

Pour yourself a cup of coffee and find your frying pan. This mason jar meal will fill your kitchen with the smell of an early Sunday morning breakfast in the South. Be prepared for some early risers when this is cookin' in the kitchen!

My parents get all the credit for letting me in on this little secret of what to do with the half-hard grits sitting on the stove leftover from breakfast. I admit I thought they were a little loony when they poured some grits into a cup and put them back in the fridge. The next morning when I woke up, I watched them turn a glob of grits into crispy golden grit cakes served straight from the skillet.

Little Miss Mason Jar likes to cook a few strips of bacon in a pan and cook the grits cakes in the bacon drippings. If bacon is not on the breakfast menu that day, butter works well. For this recipe, the jar serves as a perfect container for holding and shaping the grits until we're ready to use them. No mason jar cooking in this one. See how versatile these little jars are!

Try stacking your grits cakes with a fried egg and some crumbled bacon and green onions tossed on top. Whatever you do, get ready to experience some serious southern breakfast satisfaction when you cook these cakes.

Ingredients

2 cups cooked or leftover grits (or cheese grits)
1 egg, beaten
3 tablespoons bacon drippings or butter
Salt and pepper

Directions

1. Grease a pint size mason jar with cooking spray and fill it with grits. Put the top on the jar and place it in the refrigerator overnight.

2. When ready to make the grits cakes, take them out of the refrigerator and let them sit for ten to twenty minutes. While you wait, beat egg with salt and pepper.

3. Carefully slide the grits out of the mason jar by turning them out onto a cutting board.

4. Cut the grits into six half inch rounds.

5. Coat the grits cake in egg on both sides.

6. Cook the grits cakes in either bacon drippings or butter over medium heat for three to four minutes on each side, until golden brown.

SUNRISE PARFAIT

This mason jar breakfast meal is the perfect representation of an all American breakfast plate put in a jar. These Sunrise Parfaits can be easily assembled in the morning, sealed while piping hot and left out for hungry tummies to awake, making them the perfect grab and go breakfast.

The layers of sharp cheddar cheese in the parfait remind me of the morning sunrise creating breakfast bliss in a mason jar, telling your taste buds it is time to rise and shine.

These measurements will make two parfaits in half-pint jars. Adjust the measurements according to the number of Sunrise Parfaits you need.

Ingredients

1 cup cooked grits
2 eggs
1 tablespoon milk
$1/3$ cup sharp cheddar cheese, shredded
4 pieces cooked and crumbled bacon
Salt and pepper

Directions

Start by scrambling your eggs over medium heat with the milk and salt and pepper until cooked.

Layer the ingredients in the mason jars in this order:

¼ cup grits
2 tablespoons scrambled eggs
1 teaspoon shredded cheese
1 tablespoon bacon pieces

Repeat the layers one more time ending with bacon on top.

Screw on the lids while still hot if not serving right away.

BREAKFAST BISCUITS

You will definitely have a hard time saying good morning with a mouthful of these breakfast biscuits baked in mason jars. They are just what you need to jump start your day in a very delicious way!

Using four short half-pint mason jars works best for this recipe but tall half-pint jars will work too.

Ingredients

4 refrigerated biscuits
4 eggs
4 tablespoons cheddar cheese, shredded
4 pieces bacon or Canadian ham, cooked and cut in small pieces or crumbled
3 tablespoons milk
Salt and pepper
Flour

Directions

1. Roll out each biscuit with flour and a rolling pin until ¼ inch thick. Press biscuits into mason jars greased with cooking spray.

2. Mix egg with milk, salt, and pepper in a small bowl.

3. Sprinkle one tablespoon cheese over each biscuit. Divide egg mixture amongst the four jars evenly. Add bacon or ham to each one.

4. Cook in the oven for twelve to fourteen minutes at 400 degrees, until egg is set.

5. Remove jars from oven and let cool down for ten minutes before eating. Or pop the tops back on to seal them and store them in the refrigerator for later.

6. Remove lids and place in the microwave for twenty to thirty seconds to reheat.

CRANBERRY-ORANGE CREAM CHEESE MUFFINS

These muffins in a mason jar are hiding a surprise bite of sweet cream cheese in the middle. For a fun favor, use raffia or ribbon to dress up the mason jar and pass them out at your next Thanksgiving dinner for your guests to enjoy at breakfast the next day. They will be very thankful!

They are best when reheated in the microwave for ten to fifteen seconds before enjoying. That extra touch of warmth makes the cream cheese in the middle soft and extra delish.

Ingredients

1 box of cranberry-orange muffin mix (Krusteaz brand)
1 cup of orange juice
1 cup of fresh or frozen cranberries
6 ounces cream cheese, softened
3 tablespoons sugar

Directions

1. Prepare muffin mix as directed on the box with these two replacements: swap the water for one cup of orange juice and the canned cranberries for the fresh or frozen cranberries. After combining the mix with the orange juice, gently fold in the cranberries.

2. In a separate bowl, combine cream cheese and sugar.

3. Grease eight half-pint mason jars with cooking spray. Add $1/_3$ cup muffin batter to each jar. Drop in one heaping tablespoon cream cheese over batter. Add another $1/_3$ cup muffin batter over the cream cheese. Sprinkle with sugar and bake at 400 degrees for sixteen to eighteen minutes.

4. Carefully remove from oven and screw tops on jars to seal.

MASON JAR DO-IT-YOURSELF DRESSINGS

Making your own salad dressing is not as labor intensive as you might think. As long as you have olive oil and vinegar in your pantry you can pull off delightful do-it-yourself dressings and say goodbye to store-bought dressings filled with high fructose corn syrup and artificial flavors.

Because olive oil and vinegar do not emulsify, these Little Miss Mason Jar dressings may look a little funky after they are chilled.

Don't fret. Take the dressings out of the refrigerator before you start on dinner and let it come to room temperature. It will be back to normal in no time!

Give it a good shake when ready to dress your salad.

BASIC BALSAMIC VINAIGRETTE

This vinaigrette is the essential, basic recipe for making homemade dressings. It works well on many different salads and is the foundation for adding other ingredients to make new dressings. I keep a pint size jar of this Basic Balsamic Vinaigrette in my refrigerator and use it on almost all of my salads.

Bye, bye bottled dressings. You have been replaced.

Ingredients

$1/3$ cup olive oil
$1/3$ cup balsamic vinegar
2 teaspoons Dijon mustard
1 clove garlic, minced
1 teaspoon salt
$1/2$ teaspoon pepper

Directions

Mix all ingredients in a half-pint mason jar. Shake well.

HONEY-BALSAMIC VINAIGRETTE

I hate honey but my honey loves it. So I sneak it in recipes here and there to keep him happy. And I have to admit that I actually enjoy the subtle sweetness the honey gives this dressing. My dislike for his honey habit causes a sticky situation in our kitchen. I am trying to get my taste buds to budge but it just won't work. Hiding a little honey in our salad dressing will have to do for now.

Directions

1. Make the basic balsamic vinaigrette (page 30). Add one teaspoon honey and stir with a whisk to incorporate.
2. Store in a half-pint mason jar. Shake well before use.

RASPBERRY-BALSAMIC VINAIGRETTE

Little Miss Mason Jar loves the easy addition of raspberry preserves to perk up basic balsamic vinaigrette. The savory-sweet flavor of this dressing served with a spinach salad is a match made in mason jar heaven.

If you are using cold raspberry preserves, warm them in the microwave for ten to fifteen seconds to loosen and the dressing will be easier to mix with a smooth texture.

Directions

1. Make the basic balsamic vinaigrette (page 30). Add ¼ cup raspberry preserves and stir with a whisk to incorporate.
2. Store in a half-pint mason jar. Shake well before use.

GREEK VINAIGRETTE

Not only is this dressing perfect for Greek Orzo Pasta Salad (page 38), it is great to have on hand for when you feel like adding some feta and anchovies to your humble house salad to get a Greek vibe going. Little Miss Mason jar is no Greek Goddess but she does know a good Greek dressing when she makes one!

Ingredients

¼ cup white wine vinegar
½ cup olive oil
½ lemon, juiced
2 teaspoons lemon zest
1 teaspoon garlic powder
1 ½ teaspoons dried oregano
1 teaspoon salt
½ teaspoon pepper

Directions

Mix all ingredients in a half-pint mason jar, put the top on and shake well.

CILANTRO-LIME RANCH DRESSING

This recipe uses a store-bought dressing as a base which is usually a no-no for Little Miss Mason Jar. I have stumbled upon a wonderful ranch dressing made with all natural ingredients and no preservatives in the produce section of my grocery store. Find one that fits your likings and add a few ingredients to make a simple, semi-homemade dressing for any southwestern salad or dipping sauce.

It tastes great on Taco Salad served in mason jars (page 54).

Ingredients

1 cup ranch dressing
$1/_3$ cup fresh cilantro, chopped
1 lime, juiced
Salt and pepper to taste

Directions

1. Add all ingredients to a pint size mason jar.
2. Whisk all ingredients together.

SESAME-GINGER DRESSING

Making this dressing gives me the feeling of being in a Japanese restaurant surrounded by sushi, sake and tasty tempura. Without waiting in line for a table!

I serve this dressing with my Sesame-Ginger Tofu Salad (page 48), but it also gives a flavorful boost to a simple salad topped with crunchy chow mein noodles, peanuts or toasted sesame seeds.

Trade your apron out for a kimono, take a sip of sake and give this dressing a try. Little Miss Mason Jar promises good fortune will come your way. No cookie needed.

Ingredients

¼ cup rice wine vinegar
3 tablespoons toasted sesame oil
5 cloves garlic, minced
¼ cup soy sauce
3 teaspoons fresh ginger, grated
½ teaspoon crushed red pepper
Pinch of sugar

Directions

Mix all ingredients in a half-pint mason jar. Put the top on and shake well.

MID-DAY MASON JAR MEALS

Being an elementary school teacher means Little Miss Mason Jar's mid-day meals must be inhaled before her twenty-five minute lunch break ends. No boring brown bag lunches for me, though. Mason jar meals go from fridge to fork pronto.

Do yourself a favor and spend an hour or two on Sunday afternoon preparing mid-day mason jar meals for your work week. You will find healthy and tasty food in your fridge all week long. In addition, these help make mornings less stressful when stuffing lunches and backpacks before heading out the door.

What's not to love about that?

When assembling a salad recipe, make sure the fragile, leafy vegetables are at the top and the sturdy vegetables are in the bottom of the mason jar marinating in delicious dressing. Don't pack the Ingredients in the mason jar too tight or the dressing won't be able to coat the salad very well.

Remember, if the dressing has solidified in the refrigerator, then allow the salad to sit at room temperature for a half an hour before eating.

The beauty behind this mason jar meal is when you are ready to eat the salad, just shake it up to distribute the dressing. Eat straight from the mason jar or pour the salad into a bowl.

Hopefully, you will have longer than twenty-five minutes to enjoy a leisurely lunch made in your mason jar!

GREEK ORZO PASTA SALAD

Get a head start on your lunch for the week with this light and refreshing mason jar meal. When your stomach signals it is time for lunch, you will have this colorful, low calorie Greek Orzo Pasta Salad to satisfy you. This recipe makes six pint size mason jars, perfect for placing in the refrigerator and grabbing on your way out the door for a busy day ahead.

Ingredients

1 16-ounce box of orzo pasta
1 pint grape tomatoes, halved
1 medium cucumber, peeled and diced
6 green onions, thinly sliced
½ cup kalamata olives, sliced
¾ cup feta cheese, crumbled
 Greek Vinaigrette (page 33)

Directions

1. Boil orzo pasta in salted water according to package directions. Drain and rinse with cold water.

2. In a large bowl, mix pasta and remaining ingredients together.

3. Add the Greek vinaigrette and mix well. Season with salt and pepper.

4. Fill six pint size mason jars and place in the refrigerator overnight.

ROASTED BEET SALAD WITH GOAT CHEESE AND HONEY-BALSAMIC VINAIGRETTE

Please don't let the beets in the salad scare you away. Not only are the beets delicious when roasted with olive oil and honey, the goat cheese adds a creamy compliment to this colorful salad. Take it from Little Miss Mason Jar, this fancy and flavorful salad can't be 'beet'.

Makes five to six pint size mason jars. To make the roasted beets, mix the following Ingredients together and roast at 375 degrees for forty minutes, stirring half way through.

Ingredients

4 cups peeled and cubed beets
1 tablespoon olive oil
1 tablespoon honey
Salt and pepper

Salad Ingredients

5 cups mixed baby greens
Roasted beets
¾ cup matchstick carrots (or shredded)
6 ounces goat cheese
Honey-Balsamic Vinaigrette (page 31)
Toast ½ cup of chopped walnuts over medium-low heat for five minutes or until fragrant.

Directions

To assemble the salad, layer the following ingredients, in this order, into 5-6 pint size mason jars.

1. 1½ tablespoons Honey-Balsamic Vinaigrette at the bottom of each jar

2. ½ cup roasted beets

3. 2 tablespoons matchstick carrots (or shredded)

4. 1 tablespoon toasted walnuts

5. 2 ounces goat cheese

6. ¾ cup mixed baby greens – at the top of the jar

When you are ready to eat or serve the salad, shake it up and the dressing will mix with the salad.

PEA SALAD

Please don't turn the page just because the title of this recipe doesn't sound very tempting to your taste buds. Little Miss Mason Jar learned the hard way that this pea salad is not something to pass up when served at a potluck or backyard barbeque. For years my mom urged and advised me to taste this pea salad and for years I refused. When I finally gave in to the green, gross-sounding salad as an adult, I realized that I had been missing out on a scrumptious and savory salad.

Place this pea salad into pint size mason jars for perfect lunch portions. This recipe makes quite a bit of pea salad. Halve the recipe if you want or share a jar with your neighbors or coworkers.

Ingredients

7 cups of canned peas (we prefer LeSeur brand)
¾ block extra sharp cheddar cheese, diced
1 medium Vidalia onion, diced
4 boiled eggs, peeled and diced
½ cup mayonnaise (add up to ¼ cup more if needed)
2 teaspoons garlic powder
Salt and pepper to taste

Directions

1. Mix everything together in a large bowl and scoop into pint size mason jars.
2. Chill for a few hours or overnight.

CAPRESE SALAD

Caprese is one of Little Miss Mason Jar's all-time favorite salads. Tomato, fresh balls of mozzarella cheese, thinly sliced red onions and basil from the backyard herb garden drizzled with homemade balsamic vinaigrette delivers a sample of summer's finest with each bite. This mid-day mason jar meal is fresh, fast, and full of flavor. I make four pint size mason jars of this Caprese Salad and load them up into my lunchbox throughout the week.

Ingredients

2 pints grape tomatoes
1 container fresh mozzarella cheese balls in brine, drained and halved
1 small red onion, thinly sliced into bite size pieces
1 cup fresh basil leaves julienned
Basic Balsamic Dressing (page 30)
Salt and pepper

Directions

For each pint size jar:

1. Pour one to two tablespoons balsamic dressing in the bottom of the mason jar.
2. Add half-pint of grape tomatoes.
3. Add ¼ cup sliced red onions.
4. Distribute mozzarella cheese balls in equal amounts.
5. Top with basil leaves. Sprinkle with salt and pepper before serving.
6. Place in the refrigerator for up to a week. If the dressing is solid, let it sit on the counter for a while and the dressing will loosen up as it comes to room temperature. After the dressing softens, simply shake the dressing in the jar and serve.

SIMPLE SPINACH SALAD WITH RASPBERRY-BALSAMIC VINAIGRETTE

This simple and satisfying salad leaves Little Miss Mason Jar with a healthy feeling that lingers throughout the day. Simple Spinach Salad with Raspberry-Balsamic Vinaigrette is colorful with a little crunch from the carrots mixed with the texture of mellow mushrooms and soft eggs. The tangy raspberry vinaigrette that dresses this salad makes it stand out from the rest.

Makes four pint size jars. For larger portions, make two quart size jars.

Ingredients

4 cups fresh spinach leaves
2 cups white button mushrooms, sliced
4 eggs, boiled, peeled and sliced
½ cup shredded or thinly sliced carrots
½ cup thinly sliced red onions
Raspberry-Balsamic Vinaigrette (page 32)

Directions

Layer the salad in pint size mason jars in this order:

1. 1-2 tablespoons raspberry-balsamic vinaigrette
2. ½ cup mushrooms
3. 1 sliced egg
4. 2 tablespoons shredded carrots
5. A few red onion slices
6. 1 cup spinach leaves

Shake and serve!

SESAME-GINGER TOFU SALAD

Most people are terrified of tofu. I get it. The word tofu sounds weird, its spongy appearance is scary and the bean curd it is made from sounds sickening. But the taste of this alienated and underrated super food is quite pleasant to your palate. Put a little on your plate and you will see that there is nothing to fear. If picky Little Miss Mason Jar can eat it (and she has been for the past fifteen years), you can too!

This Sesame-Ginger Tofu Salad is filled with flavor and nutritious ingredients. It is great to have around when you feel like eating something different and your taste buds feel like traveling to a distant place. Because this salad is packed with protein, carbohydrates and fresh vegetables, it is a full meal in itself.

Makes several pint size mason jars.

Ingredients

1 package firm tofu, drained, pressed for thirty minutes and cubed
3 tablespoons soy sauce
2 tablespoons toasted sesame oil
2 tablespoons vegetable or canola oil
8 ounces buckwheat soba noodles
(udon and linguini work too)
1 large cucumber, peeled and chopped

1 cup shredded carrots
6 green onions, sliced
Sesame-Ginger Vinaigrette (page 35)

Directions

1. Drain and press tofu between several layers of paper towels on top and bottom and place a heavy object on it to press liquid out for thirty minutes. Cut tofu into one inch cubes. Combine tofu and three tablespoons soy sauce and let sit fifteen minutes, stirring gently along the way.

2. Heat two tablespoons vegetable oil and two tablespoons sesame oil over medium high heat.

3. Add tofu and cook until lightly browned all over, about seven minutes.

4. Boil soba noodles according to directions, drain and rinse with cool water.

5. In a large bowl, add soba noodles and vegetables and mix together. Add tofu and gently toss with noodles.

6. Add ½ cup Sesame-Ginger Vinaigrette and combine all ingredients together.

7. Add more dressing if needed. Salt and pepper to taste.

PRACTICAL PASTA SALAD

Preparing this pasta salad is a cinch. I came up with this recipe back in my college days when my cooking skills were basic and my budget was tight. Little Miss Mason Jar probably should have been studying for a test or writing a paper instead of playing around with pasta, but look at me now. Fifteen years later and I still remember this recipe over statistical formulas or algebraic equations. Hey, at least I was making use of math with a measuring cup!

This has become a staple in my kitchen and is a lovely lunch option during spring and summer when you want a light, refreshing meal.

I prefer this pasta salad without anything else added, but feel free to add in other ingredients to personalize it. Try small pieces of turkey pepperoni, diced rotisserie chicken breast, quartered artichoke hearts or any other veggies you have on hand.

I don't normally use bottled salad dressing but remember, this is 'practical' pasta salad and making a homemade dressing is not always practical. An olive oil based dressing such as Italian, is the way to go for me but a creamy Caesar dressing works too and makes a great Chicken-Caesar Pasta Salad.

This recipe makes about six pint size jars so make sure you have many mason jars on stand-by.

Ingredients

1 box tri-colored spiral pasta, boiled in salted water, drained and partially cooled
1 pint grape tomatoes, halved
1 medium cucumber, peeled and chopped
1 4-ounce can sliced black olives, drained
5 green onions, sliced
1 cup shredded parmesan cheese
2 cups Italian dressing
Garlic powder, salt and pepper to taste

Directions

1. In a large bowl, mix pasta, tomatoes, cucumber, olives and green onions.

2. Add parmesan cheese and dressing and mix well.

3. Add garlic powder, salt and pepper to taste.

4. Spoon into mason jars and refrigerate two or more hours, shaking a few times to keep mixture marinating in dressing.

STRAWBERRY SPINACH SALAD

When winter finally fades away and spring comes hopping by, Little Miss Mason Jar has one thing on her mind – bathing suit season. No more hibernating with cozy casseroles or backyard bonfire s'mores. The fresh feeling of spring summons salads full of flavor that won't leave you counting calories or fill you up with fat grams.

So bust out your bikini, slice some strawberries and enjoy this salad to start your season off right.

Makes four pint size mason jars.

Ingredients

4 cups spinach leaves
2 cups strawberries, sliced
1 small red onion, sliced
½ cup sunflower seeds
4 ounces feta cheese
Basic Balsamic Vinaigrette (page 30)

Directions

In each mason jar, layer the following ingredients in this order – one to two tablespoons balsamic vinaigrette, ½ cup strawberries, ¼ cup red onions, two tablespoons feta cheese, two tablespoons sunflower seeds, one cup spinach leaves.

Shake and serve.

TACO SALAD

Taco salad looks very festive with its colorful layers and tastes just as good as it looks. You won't need a sombrero or a cerveza in hand to enjoy this Mexican inspired salad made in mason jars. Mix and match the ingredients 'til your mason jar is stuffed with blissful bites of savory south of the border goodness.

For a make ahead meal, leave the ground beef cooked with taco seasoning out. Nothing is worse than cold ground beef. Little Miss Mason Jar promises you won't even miss it with the addition of protein packed kidney beans and fresh cut veggies. Pint size jars are perfect for lunch but if a bigger portion is in the plan, make it in quart size jars.

If you are serving this at your fiesta within a few hours, prep the veggies and add the spicy taco seasoned beef just before serving. Southwestern-Cilantro Ranch (page 34) pairs perfectly with this tasty taco salad. Ole!

Yields four pint size mason jars.

Ingredients

4 cups romaine lettuce, chopped

1 pint grape tomatoes, cut in half

4 green onions, sliced

6 ounces black olives, sliced

1 15-ounce can dark kidney beans, drained and rinsed

1 15-ounce can corn, drained

1 cup sharp cheddar or Monterey jack cheese, shredded

1 pound lean ground beef cooked with 1 package of taco seasoning (optional)

Fritos or tortilla chips, crumbled

Directions

1. Cook ground beef and add a package of taco seasoning according to directions (optional).

2. For a make ahead meal, layer taco salad ingredients in mason jars in this order – dressing, tomatoes, green onions, black olives, kidney beans, corn, cheese, ending with lettuce and Fritos or tortilla chips on top. If you pack it with too many ingredients, it will be hard to distribute dressing. Use a bigger jar if you are using every ingredient. If serving the salad now, let the lettuce be the first layer and add the other toppings with the dressing on top.

3. Place top on mason jar. Shake and serve.

TINY TOMATO PIES WITH BACON AND BASIL

This tasty tomato pie is made in mason jar lids. Just pop the disks through the lids like a spring form pan after the pies have cooled and there you have it — a tiny tomato pie with big bold flavors. Serve with a cup of soup on the side or a salad to complete this mid-day mason jar (lid) meal. Little Miss Mason Jar knows you will find this recipe for Tiny Tomato Pies with Bacon and Basil irresistible. They are pretty and petite and almost too cute to eat!

This recipe yields five tiny tomato pies.

Ingredients

1 refrigerated pie crust, room temperature
1 medium tomato
4 tablespoons mayonnaise or mayonnaise substitute
3 tablespoons gruyere cheese, shredded
1 tablespoon parmesan cheese, shredded
3 green onions, thinly sliced
1 teaspoon garlic powder
Salt and pepper
3 pieces of bacon, cooked and crumbled
5 fresh basil leaves, thinly sliced

Directions

1. Cut an X in the bottom of the tomato (opposite from stem). Bring a pot of water to a boil and drop tomato in for thirty seconds or until skin splits. Using tongs immediately take tomato out of boiling water and put into a bowl of ice water. Let sit in ice water for two to three minutes until cool. Remove tomato from ice water and peel the skin off starting at the X. Cut the tomato into five thin slices and place on a stack of multiple paper towels to drain excess moisture. Sprinkle with salt and pepper and let sit for fifteen minutes.

2. Unroll room temperature pie crust. Cut five circles from the pie crust by using a wide mouth lid as a template and cutting one centimeter around the edge.

3. Spray the inside of five mason jar lids with cooking spray. Gently press pie crust into prepared mason jar lids and use a fork to prick holes in the dough. Bake at 400 degrees for six minutes. Remove from oven. Place one tomato slice into each pie crust.

4. In a medium bowl, mix mayonnaise, cheeses, green onions, garlic powder, salt and pepper. Spread one heaping tablespoon of mayonnaise mixture on top of tomatoes and around edges. Sprinkle one tablespoon crumbled bacon on top.

5. Bake for ten more minutes. Remove from oven and top with strips of fresh basil.

6. Let cool five minutes before eating.

MASON JAR MUNCHIES

If it is too late for lunch and too early for dinner, mason jar munchies are just what you need to feed your snack attack. Have a handheld snack waiting on you during the day or when the midnight munchies march your way. Or invite your neighbors over and nibble on mason jar munchies while enjoying drinks on the deck.

And don't forget to invite Little Miss Mason Jar!

DILL'ICIOUS HUMMUS

A few years back my husband decided to swap out the store bought stuff for a batch of homemade hummus, adding a dash of fresh dill from our little herb garden in the backyard. Hummus happiness was created in our kitchen that day and this simple recipe has become a staple in our house ever since.

Store your hummus in a quart size mason jar or two pint size mason jars and use it throughout the week.

Here are a few of Little Miss Mason Jar's favorite ways to use hummus –

- Spread on a wrap and add your favorite sandwich ingredients
- Use it on nachos instead of refried beans
- Top it with diced tomatoes, cucumbers, kalamata olives, and feta cheese for a five layer Greek hummus dip
- Scoop some in a small mason jar and pack it on a picnic with cucumbers, carrots, and something crunchy to dip with like pretzels or pita chips

Ingredients

2 cups canned garbanzo beans, rinsed and drained
1 large clove garlic
Juice of 1 lemon
2 tablespoons tahini
1 teaspoon salt
2 tablespoons olive oil
½ cup fresh dill
Water as needed

Directions

In a food processor, chop the garlic clove. Add the garbanzo beans, dill, olive oil, salt, lemon juice and tahini. Grind until smooth. Add one tablespoon of water at a time and mix until smooth and creamy.

BOILED PEANUTS

Keep on driving past those random roadside peanut stands. I have a recipe for basic boiled peanuts to share with you today that will fill your leisurely summer days with salty bites of boiled peanut perfection.

My mom is the ruler of rounding up the best looking green peanuts around town. She has taught me a little about boiling peanuts and growing up with a pot of peanuts simmering on the stove has skilled me as well. Little Miss Mason Jar is not too proud to admit that she was raised on boiled peanuts. These boiled peanuts bring back sentimental summer memories for me. Those steamy days were spent hanging out with my family slurping peanuts from their shells and tossing them in the wind without any worries.

Bring a batch of these boiled peanuts stored in mason jars to your next baseball game, backyard bash or beach trip. You would be 'nuts' not to!

Boil the peanuts the traditional way on the stove top or cook them in a crock pot for five to seven hours, letting them sit in salt water brine for one to two hours after they are done cooking. Place peanuts in the fridge and enjoy them within a few days.

Ingredients

Fresh green peanuts
Salt
Water
Ratio: ¼ cup salt to 1 gallon peanuts

Directions

1. Using a large heavy pot, add enough water to cover the peanuts about two inches, adding more water as needed to keep them covered while cooking.

2. Add salt and boil them over medium-high heat for two to four hours, with the lid on, stirring and sampling along the way for softness.

3. When peanuts have softened, remove from heat and let them soak in the salt water for an hour or two, testing along the way until you are satisfied with the saltiness. Drain the peanuts or use a slotted spoon to scoop them into mason jars.

COWBOY CAVIAR

Saddle up, partner. I have lassoed up a recipe that will have cowboys across the country corralling cattle a little quicker to make it home for an afternoon snack. This recipe is sure to be on the most wanted list at your next get-together and will leave your guests yelling "Yee haw!"

Besides making a fantastic, finger-lickin' good snack, this recipe is also useful for topping grilled fish or chicken and would be great to use in quesadillas after being mashed with a fork and adding some Monterey Jack cheese.

Turn over a cowboy hat, fill it with chips and serve this Cowboy Caviar in true southern style!

Ingredients

1 15-ounce can corn, drained
1 15-ounce can black beans, drained and rinsed
1 15-ounce can black-eyed peas, drained and rinsed
1 red bell pepper, diced
1 small red onion, diced
½ cup cilantro, chopped

Marinade

½ cup red wine vinegar
½ cup olive oil
1 teaspoon sugar
Salt, pepper, garlic powder to taste

Directions

1. Mix corn, black beans, black eyed-peas, pepper, onion, and cilantro together in a bowl.

2. Make the marinade and pour over corn mixture. Stir well and add more salt and pepper if desired. Pour into pint or quart size mason jars.

3. Refrigerate for two to three hours or longer before serving with corn chips or Fritos.

ROASTED EGGPLANT DIP

I remember the day years ago when I watched my mom make this dip. While we gabbed over a glass of wine, she effortlessly turned a pretty purple eggplant into a bowl of delicious dip, using only a few ingredients. I didn't pay much attention until I tasted it. I was immediately impressed and asked her for the recipe in between bites.

Make this super simple recipe and store it in a mason jar for a speedy snack or easy appetizer. It also makes a good spread on a grilled veggie panini or on a portabella sandwich. No counting calories necessary when crunching away on pita chips plastered with this Roasted Eggplant Dip. This recipe is healthy and made with all natural ingredients. Little Miss Mason Jar just loves a good skinny dip!

Ingredients

2 medium eggplants
1 cup salsa
2 garlic cloves, minced
1 tablespoon olive oil
Salt and pepper to taste

Directions

1. Prick eggplant with a fork all over and bake at 375 degrees about forty-five minutes or until it collapses from the heat in the oven.

2. Let eggplant rest until cool enough to be handled. Cut in half lengthwise and scoop out the inside of the eggplant with a spoon.

3. Add salsa, garlic, and olive oil to the eggplant and mix. Season with salt and pepper.

PICKLED EGGS

If visions of Pickled Pig Feet filling up large jars at your local gas station come to mind right now please turn your thoughts to something a little more pleasant. This mason jar munchie, which is a delicious shade of purple, has a tangy taste of hard boiled eggs soaked in vinegar, beet juice and garlic cloves. Although they definitely sound a bit strange, Pickled Eggs are quite delicious when homemade and hanging out in mason jars in the refrigerator.

My maternal grandmother always enjoyed eccentric food. This random recipe is one of them. Little Miss Mason Jar cherished Pickled Eggs so much, she requested them often as a child. How many little girls do you know that beg their grandmother for Pickled Eggs?

Pickled Eggs marinating in mason jars are perfect for an Easter appetizer or an easy afternoon snack. A little sprinkle of salt makes them taste 'egg'cellent!

Yields one quart size mason jar.

Ingredients

6 hardboiled eggs, peeled
½ of a 15-ounce can sliced beets with all of the juice
1 cup apple cider vinegar
4 large garlic cloves, peeled

Directions

Place eggs and remaining ingredients in a quart size mason jar.

Refrigerate overnight

MAIN DISH MASON JAR MEALS

Toss out the take out menus cluttering your kitchen drawers. Little Miss Mason Jar is here to help you plan and prepare healthy meals for the week that leave more time for family and less mess in the sink.

Spending time on Sunday batch cooking and making main dish mason jar meals pays off in many ways.

Imagine arriving home from a hectic day at work to find a fridge full of delightful dinners, ready on the spot. If that is not tempting enough, think about all of the time you will save washing dishes during the week.

More meals and fewer dishes feel like winning the lottery to this busy working mom. Main dish mason jar meals is your winning ticket to an easier way of life.

Not even a million dollars can replace the feeling a fridge full of family dinners can!

CHICKEN POT PIE

My recipe for chicken pot pie filling is marvelous on many levels. Besides providing a delicious, easy and healthy meal for the whole family, it provides comfort with a down-home dinnertime feel.

This recipe fills two quart size mason jars, which makes two pies. In my kitchen, one jar goes into the refrigerator for the upcoming week and the other finds its way into the freezer for later. When you are ready, pour it into a pan, pop on a pie crust and dinner is done in minutes. Or you can assemble them in four pint size mason jars. Place pie crust rounds on top and bake them right away or leave them in the refrigerator for later.

Little Miss Mason Jar likes to play around with the pie dough when cutting a vent on top. A paring knife or fondant cutters are all you need to create little leaves for fall, a heart for Valentine's Day or a small star for Independence Day. Make it fun and don't be a 'chicken' when it comes to finding fun ways to dress up a plain ol' pot pie!

I have no doubt that this recipe will become a staple at your house just like it has at mine. Feel free to swap out any of the suggested vegetables with your favorite ones. A mason jar filled with this Chicken Pot Pie will fill your spoon and warm your soul.

Ingredients

1 cup carrots, finely chopped

1 cup onions, finely chopped

2 cups red potatoes, finely chopped with skin on

1 cup canned green peas

3 tablespoons butter

½ cup all-purpose flour

2 large boneless and skinless chicken breasts

2 cups chicken broth

1 cup half and half

2 teaspoons dried thyme

1 teaspoon garlic powder

2 teaspoons salt

1 teaspoon black pepper

2 refrigerated pie crusts (brought to room temperature when ready to use)

Directions

1. Boil chicken breasts in water for twenty minutes. Cool and dice into small pieces.

2. Sauté all veggies except peas in butter ten minutes. Season with salt and pepper to taste.

3. Add flour to vegetables, stirring one minute.

4. Mix chicken broth and half and half. Add to vegetable mixture and add ground thyme and garlic powder. Stir until bubbly and thick, about five minutes.

5. Add diced chicken, peas and salt and pepper. Cook over low heat five minutes. Let cool.

To Serve In Mason Jars

Spoon filling into four pint size mason jars (short work best). Use the wide mouth lid from the mason jar as a template to cut circles out of pie dough to fit the size of the jar. One pie crust yields five circles. Cut the center of the pie dough on top to vent and place in the mason jar, tucking in the pie dough and gently pushing down over the filling. Bake at 400 degrees for thirty to thirty-five minutes, until golden brown. To save for future use, place the mason jars with filling and pie crust, uncooked in the refrigerator.

Find room in the refrigerator and put a quart size mason jar full of chicken pot pie filling inside. When ready to serve, pour it into a pie plate and top with pie crust. Cut the center of the pie dough on top to vent and crimp edges. Bake at 400 degrees for thirty to forty minutes, until golden brown and bubbly.

To Freeze

Place filling in two quart size mason jars, leaving room for expansion. Thaw in refrigerator when ready to use. Pour into a pie plate and top with pie crust. Cut the center of the pie dough on top to vent and crimp edges. Bake at 400 degrees for thirty to forty minutes, until golden brown and bubbly.

SHEPHERD'S PIE

Little Miss Mason Jar is not Irish but she does love a good piece of Shepherd's Pie every now and then. Besides luring in the luck of the Irish on Saint Patrick's Day with this recipe, I love to make this comforting and filling meal many times throughout the year. If you don't have time to fool with the do-it-yourself broth and flour gravy that thickens up the beef mixture, substitute one jar of beef flavored gravy instead.

This recipe makes four-five pint size jars.

Ingredients

1 lb. lean ground beef
1 medium onion, diced
1 cup beef broth
1 tablespoon all-purpose flour
1 tablespoon tomato paste
1 teaspoon garlic powder
1 cup frozen corn
1 cup frozen peas and carrots
3 cups mashed potatoes
1 ¼ cup shredded sharp cheddar cheese
Salt and pepper to taste

Directions

1. To make the meat mixture, cook beef and onion together until beef is cooked and no longer pink. Mix beef broth and flour together and add to meat mixture. Simmer over medium-low heat for one minute. Add tomato paste, garlic powder and salt and pepper to taste. Continue cooking for two minutes, stirring along the way.

2. Layer the ingredients in this order. The meat mixture should be at the bottom of the jar and the cheese at the top.

   - Meat mixture
   - Corn
   - Peas and carrots
   - Mashed potatoes
   - Cheddar cheese

3. Place a cookie sheet in the oven and place the jars on the cookie sheet to bake at 375 degrees for twenty-five to thirty minutes.

4. Let cool for ten to fifteen minutes before serving. To make this ahead, store in the refrigerator for up to four days before baking.

CHILI WITH CORNBREAD

As soon as signs of fall start to arrive and the first cold snap summoning a sweater appears on my doorstep, I start to crave a big bowl of chili. Little Miss Mason Jar has come a long way from opening a can of chili starter and adding ground beef and a can of tomatoes to create an instant pot of piping hot chili. And while I am not a huge fan of cornbread, it is hard to deny that chili and cornbread make a perfect partnership in creating a hearty and wholesome meal to warm you up when summer says goodbye and cold weather wanders near.

Grab a sweater and stir up a fun twist on a traditional bowl of chili with crumbly cornbread on the side by combining them both in a mason jar and cooking in the oven.

This recipe makes four pint size mason jars and leaves lots of leftover chili.

Ingredients

1 cup onion, chopped
¾ cup green bell pepper, chopped (any color pepper will do)
2 cloves of garlic, minced (or 1 tablespoon prepared garlic/garlic powder)
1 pound lean ground beef
1 15-ounce can black beans, drained and rinsed
1 15-ounce can kidney beans, drained and rinsed
1 15-ounce can hominy, drained
1 14-ounce can of diced tomatoes with juice
1 tablespoon chili powder
1 tablespoon cumin

½ teaspoon salt
½ teaspoon pepper
2 ½ cups beef broth

For The Cornbread

1 8.5-ounce package of cornbread mix
¾ cup corn (canned or frozen)
1 cup Monterey Jack cheese, shredded
3 green onions, sliced
¾ cup of milk
1 egg

Directions

1. Cook onion, pepper, garlic and ground beef over medium-high heat for ten minutes or until beef is no longer pink and vegetables are soft. Drain grease if needed.
2. Return beef mixture to a large pot and add the remaining ingredients (beans through broth). Simmer over medium-low heat for fifteen minutes.
3. In a bowl, stir cornbread mix, corn, cheese, green onions, milk and egg.
4. Carefully spoon chili into pint size mason jars, filling half way.
5. Add $\frac{1}{3}$ cup cornbread mix to the mason jars.
6. Bake chili and cornbread in the oven at 400 degrees for fifteen to twenty minutes or until cornbread is golden brown.
7. Remove from oven carefully and let sit for ten minutes before serving.

EASY ENCHILADA FILLING

If you are looking for a way to spice things up with your weekly menu, try to incorporate Mexican Monday or Fiesta Friday. Having theme nights to guide your grocery list is a fun way to keep things exciting with little effort. Start with some chips, salsa and cerveza and let this mason jar meal do the rest.

This recipe is very versatile and lends itself to traditional enchiladas rolled up and baked until bubbly, put together as an enchilada pie or stuffed into taco shells and baked in the oven.

Make this filling on Sunday when you are cooking for the week ahead and put it in a quart size mason jar until you need it. Little Miss Mason Jar suggests making Southwestern-Cilantro Coleslaw (page 83) to go with your easy enchiladas.

Ingredients

For the filling

1 15-ounce can of refried beans
1 cup sharp cheddar cheese, shredded
¾ cup salsa

Additional Ingredients

4-5 flour tortillas
1 10-ounce can enchilada sauce (red or green)
1 cup of sharp cheddar cheese or Monterey Jack, shredded
½ cup tomatoes, diced
½ cup green onions, sliced
Sour cream (optional)

ENCHILADAS

1. Spread ½ cup of filling on each tortilla.

2. Roll up and place seem down in a 9x9 baking dish.

3. Pour enchilada sauce over tortillas and sprinkle cheese evenly over the top.

4. Cover with foil and bake at 375 degrees for twenty minutes or until sauce is bubbling. Remove the foil and return to oven for five more minutes.

5. Serve enchiladas with diced tomatoes, green onions and sour cream on top.

ENCHILADA PIE

1. Place one tortilla in the bottom of a pie pan coated with cooking spray. Spread ½ cup of filling onto tortilla and top with another tortilla. Spread $\frac{1}{3}$ cup of enchilada sauce over the top tortilla.

2. Continue layering tortillas, filling, and enchilada sauce, ending with a tortilla on top and covered with enchilada sauce.

3. Sprinkle more cheese over the top and cover with foil.

4. Bake at 325 degrees for twenty minutes. Remove foil and bake for five more minutes.

5. Sprinkle diced tomatoes and green onions on top of the pie. Cut into wedges and serve with a scoop of sour cream on top.

ENCHILADA OVEN BAKED TACOS

Additional Ingredients

Eight hard taco shells

Taco sauce

Directions

1. Stuff $1/3$ cup enchilada filling into hard taco shells and place them together so they are touching in a small square baking dish.

2. Sprinkle Monterey Jack cheese on tacos and bake in the oven at 350 degrees for ten minutes.

3. Spread some taco sauce on the tacos and top with green onions, diced tomatoes and sour cream.

SOUTHWESTERN-CILANTRO COLESLAW

Store this south of the border coleslaw recipe in two quart size mason jars or four pint size.

Ingredients

6 cups shredded coleslaw mix
4 green onions, sliced
½ cup cilantro, chopped
4 tablespoons mayonnaise or mayonnaise substitute
Juice of 1 lime
1 teaspoon cumin
1 teaspoon garlic powder
1 teaspoon salt
½ teaspoon pepper

Directions

1. Mix coleslaw, green onions and cilantro together in a large bowl.

2. In a small bowl, whisk mayonnaise and next five ingredients together.

3. Pour mayonnaise mixture over coleslaw mix and combine. Season with more salt to taste.

4. Chill in the refrigerator for an hour or longer.

MASON JAR MEATLOAF

Meatloaf gets a bad rap sometimes. Maybe it is because of its mushy, mystery meat appearance. Or maybe it brings back bad memories of school cafeteria lunch and the lingering smell of meatloaf and broccoli drifting out the doors and down the halls of the school. Well, Little Miss Mason Jar is about to change that.

This meatloaf, made with sharp cheddar cheese and rolled oats, will change your mind in minutes and erase any previous pessimistic meatloaf-related feelings you may have had in the past. Made directly in mason jars, this meatloaf puts a modern twist on an old classic. Alternatively, this meatloaf mixture can be stored in a quart size mason jar and made the traditional way.

This recipe makes six half-pint mason jar meatloaves or three pint size.

Ingredients

½ cup ketchup
¼ cup mustard
2 heaping tablespoons brown sugar
I pound lean ground beef
I small onion, diced
I cup quick cook oats

I cup sharp cheddar cheese, shredded
¾ cup milk
I egg, beaten
I tablespoon garlic powder
Salt and pepper to taste

Directions

1. In a small bowl mix ketchup, mustard and brown sugar.

2. In a large bowl combine ground beef and remaining ingredients. Add half of ketchup mixture and combine with hands. Add salt and pepper to taste.

3. Fill the mason jars ¾ of the way with meatloaf mixture. Spread remaining ketchup mixture on top.

4. Bake in the oven at 375 degrees for fifty to sixty minutes. Let cool ten minutes before serving.

5. If you are making these ahead of time seal the mason jars and store them in the refrigerator before baking. Bake when ready to serve.

MASON JAR MAC AND CHEESE WITH SPINACH, BACON AND MUSHROOMS

Little Miss Mason Jar has had to learn the hard way – no matter how many homemade macaroni and cheese meals you present to children, they prefer the powdered cheese kind that costs under a buck and tastes like the cardboard blue box it comes in. Well, no more trying to force feed fancy mac and cheese to four year olds. I give up.

So grownups, gather around. This macaroni and cheese covered with a creamy cheese sauce, baked with spinach, bacon, and mushrooms and topped with panko bread crumbs and parmesan cheese is for you. Boil a box of boring, bland macaroni and cheese for the kids. This version is rich and flavorful and laced with bits of bacon and earthy mushrooms. Freshly grated gruyere and Swiss cheese take this big kid mac and cheese main dish meal to another level.

This recipe can be baked straight in a mason jar, stored in the refrigerator or frozen for future use. Prepare for a pot full of macaroni and cheese that fills many mason jars. Fill half-pint mason jars for lunch portions and pint size mason jars for main dish dinners. Or use quart size mason jars to contain the mac and cheese in the freezer, thaw when ready and cook in a casserole dish.

Ingredients

2½ cups uncooked macaroni noodles
4 slices of bacon, divided
¾ cup onion, diced
2 cups mushrooms, diced
3 cups fresh spinach leaves, chopped
4 tablespoons butter
4 tablespoons flour

3½ cups milk
1½ cup gruyere cheese, shredded
1 cup Swiss cheese, shredded
1½ teaspoons ground mustard
½ cup panko crumbs
½ cup parmesan cheese, grated
Salt and pepper

Directions

1. Boil pasta in salted water until al dente. Pasta should be a little undercooked. Drain.
2. Cook bacon in a pan. Remove from pan and drain grease, reserving one tablespoon in the pan.
3. Sauté onions and mushrooms in bacon drippings, five minutes. Add spinach and sauté until spinach wilts. Add salt and pepper to taste.
4. In a large pot, melt butter over medium heat. Add flour and whisk until combined, one to two minutes. Pour in milk and stir. Add ground mustard and salt and pepper.
5. Stir in gruyere and Swiss cheese. Continue to simmer over low heat while stirring until cheese melts completely.
6. Add pasta, mushroom mixture and four pieces of crumbled bacon to cheese sauce. Stir well. Add salt and pepper to taste.
7. Let cool, stirring a few times along the way.
8. In a bowl, mix panko crumbs and parmesan cheese for the topping.

To Make In Mason Jars

Divide mac and cheese mixture among mason jars. Sprinkle two tablespoons panko-parmesan topping over macaroni mixture. Bake at 375 degrees for twenty minutes. Let cool five to ten minutes.

To Store for Later

Place mac and cheese filled mason jars in the refrigerator or freezer before adding topping. If frozen, thaw before baking. Add two tablespoons topping to each mason jar and bake at 375 degrees for twenty minutes. Let cool five to ten minutes.

BARBEQUE PULLED PORK PARFAIT (WITH ALL THE FIXIN'S)

Take a seat around the table. Little Miss Mason Jar has prepared a southern staple with a sophisticated twist that is sure to surprise even the biggest barbeque buff in the South. This Barbeque Pulled Pork Parfait piles beer infused baked beans with crispy coleslaw and perfectly pulled pork. Cubes of garlic toast are tossed on top with a drizzle of barbeque sauce to finish. Nothing like a mason jar main meal that bottles the flavors of a plate piled high with barbeque and all the fixin's!

The ingredient list may look a little overwhelming at first. But considering the pork cooks in a crock pot all day and the sides are simple to make, this mason jar meal is not much work at all. And here is a little secret- A local barbeque restaurant is the answer to your prayers if you do not have time to make this recipe from scratch. Call in a takeout order of pulled pork, baked beans, coleslaw and garlic toast to build a barbeque parfait the easy way.

PULLED PORK

2½ pound Boston butt, cut in 3 large pieces   I large onion, sliced

DRY RUB

Mix all ingredients in a half-pint mason jar and store leftovers in the pantry.

¼ cup paprika   I tablespoon ground mustard
I tablespoon salt   I tablespoon brown sugar
I tablespoon pepper   I tablespoon onion powder
I tablespoon garlic powder   I teaspoon cayenne pepper

HONEY BARBEQUE SAUCE

Simmer all ingredients over medium heat until thick and bubbly and slightly reduced.

½ cup ketchup

1 tablespoon mustard

½ cup apple cider vinegar

1 teaspoon Worcestershire sauce

$1/8$ teaspoon cayenne pepper

1 tablespoon honey

¼ teaspoon red pepper flakes

1 teaspoon salt

½ teaspoon pepper

Directions

1. Place sliced onions in crock pot. Coat pieces of pork in $1/3$ cup dry rub and pat firmly. Place on top of onions. Pour half of the barbeque sauce on the pork and cook on low heat eight hours.

2. Remove pork and onions from crock pot and let rest five minutes. Shred meat and onions. Add shredded meat mixture to the reserved barbeque sauce and cook over low heat until heated through.

BAKED BEANS

2 15-ounce cans navy beans, drained and rinsed
1 cup green bell pepper, diced
1 cup barbeque sauce

½ cup beer (optional)
2 tablespoons dark brown sugar
1 tablespoon Worcestershire sauce
Salt and pepper to taste

Directions

1. Mix all ingredients together and pour into an 8 inch baking dish.
2. Bake, uncovered at 375 degrees forty-five to fifty minutes.

CLASSIC COLESLAW

Ingredients

16 ounce bag coleslaw mix
3 green onions, sliced
4 heaping tablespoons mayonnaise or
mayonnaise substitute
1 tablespoon apple cider vinegar

1 teaspoon onion powder
1 teaspoon sugar
1 teaspoon salt
½ teaspoon pepper

Directions

1. Combine coleslaw mix and green onions.

2. In a small bowl, whisk mayonnaise and next five ingredients.

3. Pour mayonnaise mixture over coleslaw mix and stir well.

4. Refrigerate one hour or longer.

Make garlic toast or heat frozen garlic toast according to package directions. Cut into cubes.

TO BUILD THE BARBEQUE PULLED PORK PARFAIT

Layer the ingredients in pint size mason jars in the following order – baked beans, coleslaw, pulled pork, garlic toast cubes. Drizzle barbeque sauce on top.

JACKIE O'S PENNE PASTA WITH VODKA SAUCE

Little Miss Mason Jar has an aunt who is a lot like she is. We share the same first name, love the color yellow, are terrified of frogs and lizards and we both love to cook. Years ago, when snail mail was still the way of the world, Aunt Jackie and I decided to write each other letters and share recipes from time to time.

One of her envelopes sent from South Carolina contained a sweet letter and her recipe for Penne Pasta with Vodka Sauce. This recipe is a favorite for us both and a flavorful reminder of a trip we took to Maine where she first taught me how to make it.

Of course, I couldn't resist turning this family favorite into a mason jar meal. Each jar of Jackie O's Penne Pasta with Vodka Sauce brings a taste of Italy to your kitchen in no time. A salad served alongside, a basket of bread and a glass of vino complete this easy and elegant mason jar meal.

Ingredients

1 8-ounce box Penne pasta, cooked and drained
1 28-ounce can Stewed Tomatoes
1 medium onion, diced
1 large garlic clove, minced
2 tablespoons olive oil
½ teaspoon crushed red pepper flakes

½ cup vodka (Skip if you want or replace with red wine if you can't handle the strong stuff!)
½ cup room temperature heavy cream or half and half
Salt and pepper
Grated Parmesan cheese and fresh basil leaves for garnish

Directions

1. Sauté onion and garlic in olive oil until soft.

2. Add tomatoes and simmer on medium-low for twenty to thirty minutes. Add red pepper flakes, stir and cook another five minutes. Stir in vodka and simmer another fifteen minutes on low.

3. Stir in cream. Cook one to two minutes until heated through. Season with salt and pepper. Let cool.

Layer pint size mason jars in the following order: penne pasta, vodka sauce, grated parmesan cheese and strips of fresh basil. Enjoy right away or reheat when ready. If you prefer not to eat this from mason jars, assemble the ingredients upside down in several pint or quart size mason jars—vodka sauce on the bottom and penne pasta on top. When you pour the pasta out of the jar the sauce will be on top. Reheat then sprinkle grated parmesan cheese and strips of fresh basil.

CREAMY CORN CHOWDER

This soup is hearty and flavorful and comes from my mother-in-law's kitchen. The cream cheese takes this soup from good to great and makes it delicious beyond words. I always have a batch brewing in my crock pot for our fall festivities. You should too!

Store this soup in several mason jars to fit your needs. Quart size for dinner portions, pint size for a lighter lunch option.

Ingredients

1 roll Jimmy Dean Sausage with Sage
1 onion, diced
3 large white potatoes, peeled and cubed
1 32-ounce box chicken broth

1 15-ounce can corn, drained
1 15-ounce can cream corn
6 ounces of cream cheese, softened
Salt and pepper to taste

Directions

1. In a large pot, cook and crumble sausage until brown. Remove sausage from pan using a slotted spoon.

2. Cook onions in sausage drippings for five minutes over medium heat.

3. Add potatoes and chicken broth and bring to a boil. Reduce heat to medium and cook for seven to ten minutes, until potatoes are tender.

4. Add corn, cream corn, and sausage to pot and simmer five minutes.

5. Add cream cheese and cook, stirring often, until cheese is melted, about ten minutes.

6. Salt and pepper to taste.

SOMETHING TO SIP ON

Sipping from mason jars makes life fun. I know - I don't get out much. But, there is something nostalgic about drinking out of mason jars. It brings out smiles and a sense of unity among the past and the present. As my grandmother-in-law tells me, there once was a time when all there was to drink from was mason jars.

She chuckles at the mason jar mania that has taken over the world and reminds me of days past when mason jars were not so glamorous. They were just glass jars used for everyday living. No big deal. Well, times have changed but one thing has not – mason jars are convenient for sipping and storing drinks no matter what decade it is.

Pack a picnic basket with half-pints of wine or make Bloody Marys as you head out the door to enjoy a sunset at the beach. Pour, seal, sip – that's all there is to it! From lemonade to liquid libations, mason jars are ideal for travel and for cramming in the cooler so you will have something to drink when you reach your destination.

VANILLA ICED COFFEE

It is no secret Little Miss Mason Jar loves coffee. Two cups in the morning and sometimes an afternoon pick me up or late night jolt of caffeine is normal; or should I say necessary. During the summer I like my afternoon cup of coffee cold. So I make a little extra in the morning and pour the leftovers in a mason jar and cool it in the refrigerator. When fatigue finds its way into my afternoon packed with plans I create this coffee drink to keep me moving. Skip the Starbucks drive through, you will like it a latte!

Store this vanilla iced coffee in four half-pint mason jars. When you are craving caffeine, take off the top and start sipping.

Ingredients

3 cups cold strong coffee
½ cup milk
½ cup half and half

2 tablespoons sugar
½ teaspoon vanilla

Directions

1. Mix all ingredients together and stir with a whisk.
2. Pour into mason jars. Drink immediately or put the top on and store in the refrigerator for a few days.

PUMPKIN PIE COFFEE CREAMER

Why buy expensive flavored coffee from a drive through window or purchase factory made flavored coffee creamer when you could make your own at home? This recipe for Pumpkin Pie Coffee Creamer will sweeten your coffee and save you money. Little Miss Mason Jar has no doubt you will 'fall' in love with this recipe!

Ingredients

1 cup whole milk
¾ cup half and half
4 tablespoons pumpkin puree
1 teaspoon pumpkin pie spice
1 teaspoon vanilla
1 teaspoon sugar (more if desired)

Directions

1. Cook milk, half and half and pumpkin puree over medium heat until warm, stirring with a whisk. Do not boil.

2. Remove from heat and add pumpkin pie spice, vanilla and sugar. Whisk well.

3. Let cool and store in a pint size mason jar. Shake well before use.

CRANBERRY SPRITZER

This cranberry cocktail was concocted during a cranberry craze I went through a few years back. With cranberries covering my kitchen countertops and a bottle of wine waiting in the fridge, it was bound to happen.

Fill half-pint mason jars to the brim with this Cranberry Spritzer and keep them on ice for family and friends at Thanksgiving dinner. Little Miss Mason Jar likes to roll damp cranberries in sugar and freeze them on a tray to use in place of ice. Talk about a Happy Thanksgiving!

Ingredients

1 ½ cups white wine (sauvignon blanc or riesling)
1 ½ cups cranberry-apple juice
1 cup sparkling water
Fresh cranberries rolled in sugar and frozen for garnish
Apple wedges for garnish

Directions

Combine wine, cranberry juice and sparkling water. Stir well.

LUSCIOUS LEMONADE

When I received my grandmother's retro electric juicer from years past, I was reluctant to use it. It was old and ugly. In my mind there was no way it would work as well as the lime green KitchenAid juicer that was on my kitchen wish list. Well, for once in my life, I am proud to announce that I was wrong. Way wrong! All it took was half of a lemon and I was in love. And I was also feeling pretty guilty for giving the old juicer a hard time in the first place. If it was good enough for my grandmother, then it was good enough for Little Miss Mason Jar.

Fill up half-pint or pint-size mason jars, pop the tops on and leave them chilling in the refrigerator or cooler. For a grown up Cherry-Lemonade libation, add a little vodka, a splash of maraschino cherry juice and of course, a cherry!

Save the empty lemon halves and place tea lights in them to chase away the backyard mosquitoes or add a scoop of raspberry sorbet to the little lemon bowl that is left after juicing it.

Ingredients

2 cups sugar
2 cups water

10 lemons (enough for 2 cups lemon juice)
8 cups water

Directions:

1. Make simple syrup by combining the sugar and two cups water in a small saucepan. Bring to a low boil and simmer until all sugar is dissolved and the water is clear and thick. Place in a mason jar and in the refrigerator until cool.
2. Cut the lemons in half and juice them to equal two cups.
3. Combine the simple syrup, lemon juice and eight cups of water. Allow time to chill in the refrigerator before drinking.

SANGRIA SIPPER

There is something about Sangria that brings out a smile in everyone. And Little Miss Mason Jar isn't talking about the alcohol content! This Sangria recipe is refreshing and the Sprite gives it a little fizz. To help prevent the Sangria from getting watered down, freeze lemon wedges and use in place of ice.

Note: The Sprite will cause this drink to go flat so be prepared to drink the whole amount or add a splash of sprite to your sangria before serving individually to help keep the drink fresh.

Ingredients

3 cups lemonade (recipe on page 101 or use store bought)
1 cup orange juice
$1/3$ cup sugar
3 cups burgundy wine
½ cup Brandy
3 cups Sprite soda

Directions

1. Mix all ingredients except Sprite. Chill until ready to serve.
2. Before serving, add Sprite and pour into pint size mason jars with frozen lemon wedges.

MASON JAR SWEETS AND TREATS

Savory mason jar meals aren't the only thing Little Miss Mason Jar has mastered. Sweets and treats made in mason jars have become my favorite way to showcase decadent desserts and terrific little treats. Desserts displayed in mason jars make them easy to dole out and are portion controlled.

So go ahead and indulge in a sweet treat tucked away in a mason jar. Everyone needs to spoil their sweet tooth from time to time and what better way to do it than with a make ahead mason jar dessert.

BLUEBERRY SUGAR COOKIE COBBLER

This after-supper, sweet treat is made with only four ingredients. It screams summertime and is perfect for dessert on the porch after a delicious dinner. You can assemble this mason jar dessert ahead of time and refrigerate them for a few hours before baking. Store any leftovers (I doubt you will have any!) in the refrigerator and unscrew the tops and microwave them for twenty to thirty seconds to reheat.

Make sure you have vanilla ice cream close by, which pairs perfectly with this burst of blueberry heaven in a jar! This recipe makes four pint size mason jars or six half-pint mason jars.

Ingredients

2 cups fresh or frozen blueberries
¾ cup blueberry pie filling (such as Comstock)
$1/_3$ cup sugar
1 roll refrigerated prepared sugar cookie dough

Directions

1. Mix blueberries, pie filling and sugar in a bowl.

2. Add blueberry mixture to the mason jars and fill half way.

3. Crumble sugar cookie dough over the blueberry mixture to fill jars ¾ of the way.

4. Cover each jar with foil and bake at 350 degrees for fifteen minutes. Carefully remove the foil and return to the oven for another fifteen minutes or until golden brown. If needed, broil for two to three minutes.

5. Allow to cool for ten to fifteen minutes before serving with a scoop of vanilla ice cream right in the jar!

PUMPKIN PIE CRUNCH

Little Miss Mason Jar can pass up pumpkin pie with ease. But this recipe puts ordinary pumpkin pie to shame with a crunchy topping and fantastic flavor. This will become a fast favorite in your house when cooler weather comes a knockin'. It also makes a dainty and delicious dessert for your Thanksgiving menu. The color of the rustic orange pumpkin pie filling buried beneath a golden brown layer of crisp cake and pecans lets this mason jar dessert speak for itself.

Go ahead and put your previous pumpkin pie recipe away. You won't need it anymore after you taste this!

This recipe yields ten half-pint mason jars (short work best).
It is best served warm with whipped cream, Cool Whip, or a scoop of vanilla ice cream and a sprinkle of cinnamon on top or a fancy cinnamon stick for garnish.

Ingredients

1 15-ounce can solid pack pumpkin
1 and ½ cups sugar
1 12-ounce can evaporated milk
3 eggs

4 teaspoons pumpkin pie spice
½ teaspoon salt
1 box butter flavored cake mix
1 cup chopped pecans
1 cup butter, melted

Directions

1. Preheat oven to 350 degrees and grease mason jars with cooking spray.

2. Combine pumpkin, eggs, evaporated milk, sugar, pumpkin pie spice, and salt with a whisk.

3. Pour into the greased mason jars to fill half way.

4. Sprinkle two tablespoons dry cake mix evenly over the pumpkin mixture. Top with one tablespoon chopped pecans. Drizzle two tablespoons melted butter over pecans.

5. Bake for fifty to sixty minutes, until golden brown. Refrigerate leftovers. To reheat, remove the lids and cook in microwave for twenty to thirty seconds.

MASON JAR MUD PIE

When I think of mud pie, I don't get thoughts of a chocolate crusted coffee ice cream pie slathered with sweet chocolate sauce and whipped cream on top. Nope. Not at all. Instead, I take a trip back in time to my childhood when my siblings and I would go off on a summer adventure around the neighborhood and down the dirt road that was our childhood playground. Many memories were made as we filled our long, lazy summer days with go-cart driving, fort building, fish catching, fossil finding and sometimes an occasional dare or two just to keep things exciting.

One day, my daredevil of a sister had a different recipe for mud pie than the traditional and tasty one I have for you here. Her recipe for mud pie consisted of freshly made mud leftover from a daily downpour of afternoon rain that comes during summertime in Florida. As we sat down on the wet dirt road, picking up pebbles and preparing pretend dinner made out of mud a dare came out of nowhere. "I'll give you fifty cents if you lick that." my brother said, pointing down at her massive mud pie. "I'll lick it for free!" she said, and proceeded to do just that. With a smile on her face and lots of laughs from the kid-filled crowd, we made a great memory that day to never be forgotten and gets told every now and then just as a reminder that when life hands you mud, make mud pie. Preferably this recipe!

This recipe makes four half-pint mason jars. Wide mouth short mason jars work best.

Ingredients

1 cup Oreo cookies crushed in a food processor (about eleven cookies)
2 tablespoons butter, melted
2 cups coffee ice cream, softened
1 12-ounce jar of hot fudge sundae topping (heated according to directions)
1 can whipped cream

Directions

1. Mix crushed cookies and melted butter together. Add two tablespoons of cookie crumbs to the bottom of each jar and use the back of the spoon to press down to cover the bottom. Place in the freezer for one hour.

2. Add two scoops of softened ice cream to the jars and use your fingers to press it down to cover the cookie crumbs. Add one more scoop of ice cream and press down again.

3. Pour two tablespoons hot fudge sauce over ice cream.

4. Seal the jars and put them in the freezer for at least three hours before serving.

5. When ready to serve, remove from the freezer and let sit for five to ten minutes. Add whipped cream and another drizzle of chocolate syrup to the top.

COOKIES AND CREAM CUPCAKES

Little Miss Mason Jar just loves this cute cupcake in a jar idea. Besides being simple and scrumptious, they are so adorable! These are perfect for passing out as party favors, serving at birthday parties, packing on a picnic or bringing to a bake sale.

When it comes to cupcakes and frosting, Little Miss Mason Jar likes to make her own. I use a box cake mix and substitute the oil or water with the same measurements of milk or buttermilk and add a bit of vanilla for a more homemade taste. You can add anything from pudding to sour cream to powdered pink lemonade or crushed cookies to make a cake mix come to life. And while I am not a fan of food coloring, it does have its place in my pantry for baking purposes. For frosting, you should make the extra effort and mix up a batch of your own. The process is practically effortless and the results are worth it. There are many things you can add to frosting to kick up the flavor as well, so get creative in your kitchen and do it in Little Miss Mason Jar style. If you absolutely can't find it in yourself to bust out your inner Little Miss Mason Jar, order unfrosted cupcakes and a pound of frosting from your local bakery and go from there.

To make sure you have the perfect size cupcakes, add ¼ cup of batter to each cupcake liner to ensure they won't come out with a raised surface. It is best to have them flat.
For this recipe I am using plain vanilla cupcakes. Feel free to add more crushed cookies to your cake batter or use chocolate cupcakes instead. Your kitchen, your call!

And now for a really cool tip (pun intended!) – cupcakes and frosting freeze wonderfully. I can rest easier at night knowing I have a dozen cupcakes and a mason jar full of frosting in my freezer to bust out at any time I am in a baking bind. This recipe yields eight tall half-pint mason jars.

Ingredients

1½ cups Oreo cookies crushed in a food processor (approximately fifteen cookies)
4 cups vanilla butter cream frosting
12 unfrosted vanilla cupcakes cut in half horizontally

Directions

1. In a bowl, stir cookie crumbs into frosting.
2. Place one piece of cupcake in a mason jar and gently push to the bottom. Fill a pastry bag or zip top bag with frosting and cut a hole in the corner. Pipe about two tablespoons frosting onto the cupcake.
3. Place another cupcake piece on top of the frosting. Pipe more frosting on top of the cupcake. Add one more layer of cupcake and frosting for three layers of each.
4. These should be stored in the fridge if using fresh frosting. Take them out to soften up an hour or so before eating.

BASIC VANILLA BUTTERCREAM FROSTING

Ingredients

1 stick butter, softened
3¾ cups powdered sugar, sifted
2 teaspoons vanilla extract
3 tablespoons milk

Directions

1. Using a mixer, beat softened butter thirty seconds.
2. Turn off the mixer and add powdered sugar, vanilla, and milk. Beat on low for thirty seconds then turn the mixer to medium and beat until frosting is creamy. Add one or two more tablespoons of milk to thin out if needed.

Little Miss Mason Jar has More Tricks for Making Adorable Mason Jar Cupcakes

- Tint cream cheese frosting green and layer with red velvet cupcakes for Christmas
- Tint cream cheese frosting pink and layer with red velvet cupcakes for Valentine's Day
- Tint cake batter red and blue and use white vanilla butter cream frosting for the Fourth of July
- Tint frosting orange and layer with dark chocolate cupcakes for Halloween

PEANUT BUTTER AND JELLY JARS

What do you get when you put peanut butter and jelly with sweet sugar cookie dough, crunchy granola and peanut butter morsels in a mason jar and bake it in the oven? A 'jam' up jar of pure peanut butter and jelly pleasure. Don't forget a scoop of vanilla ice cream right in the jar to really tempt your taste buds.

Short, half-pint mason jars work best. The recipe makes six half-pint mason jars.

Ingredients

1 roll of refrigerated sugar cookie dough, divided
1 cup grape jelly (any flavor works)
¾ cup plain granola
¾ cup peanut butter morsels

Directions

1. Use ⅔ of the roll of sugar cookie dough. Save remaining $^1/_3$ dough. Grease mason jars with cooking spray. Divide dough evenly in jars and press into the bottoms of greased mason jars to fill about ½ inch in each.

2. Spread two tablespoons jelly over dough.

3. In a bowl, mix remaining sugar cookie dough with granola and peanut butter chips. Lightly press ⅓ cup of granola mixture over jelly.

4. Carefully put in oven at 375 degrees for twenty to thirty minutes until golden brown.

5. Seal immediately and listen for the popping sound while they cool. Place in the refrigerator for two or more hours. When ready to serve, let them come to room temperature or remove lids and reheat in the microwave for twenty to thirty seconds. These will last four or five days in the fridge.

STRAWBERRY SHORTCAKE

The inspiration for this delightful dessert in a jar comes from a children's birthday party I attended that had a picnic theme. My inner party planner came creeping out and I was busy doting on every little detail like blankets laid on the lawn and perfect picnic cuisine. Little did I know, the host was saving the best sweet touch for last. In addition to a cute cake created to look like a picnic basket with ants crawling across, she was serving strawberry shortcake in mason jars. My jaw dropped and my mouth opened wide when I saw the tray in her hand. I am not sure if saliva was dripping from my mouth at that point, but I really didn't care. I was only focused on one thing, having the host reveal the recipe. Luckily for me (and you) she did.

For the Fourth of July holiday, add blueberries tossed with sugar to the mix for a Patriotic Parfait. It is the perfect finish to a day full of family, friends, fun and fireworks.

These can be made ahead of time and chilled until ready to be served. Make sure to let them sit at room temperature for about thirty minutes to take off the chill. Go light on the amount of Ingredients you add so you can fit at least two layers in the jars for best results. One layer works too if you find yourself with a heavy hand. It happens.

This recipe makes six to seven half-pint mason jars or four pint size mason jars.

Ingredients

1 package of strawberries, rinsed and thinly sliced

2 tablespoons sugar

1 pound cake (purchased from bakery or frozen section and thawed)

1 regular size container of Cool Whip, thawed

10 ounces vanilla frosting (¾ of tub)

Directions

1. Gently stir strawberries and sugar together in a bowl. Cover and let sit thirty minutes or longer.

2. Mix Cool Whip and frosting together.

3. Cut pound cake into small cubes.

4. Layer the ingredients in the mason jars as follows—pound cake, strawberries, Cool Whip mixture. Then repeat ingredients to fill the jars.

MASON JAR FUDGE PIE

Put your pie plate away and make room for mason jars. This recipe may change the way you prepare pies for the rest of your life. First, make a quick batch of chocolate fudge filling. From here you have two tasty choices for how to make your pretty little pies.

You can bake your pie in mason jars or you can bake your pie using mason jar lids and you will have mini chocolate pies. Keep the mini chocolate pie in the lid and wrap in a clear cellophane bag tied with twine to give to someone else or for favors at a party. To release the pies, push up on the bottom of the lid and hold on to the ring. Out pops a tiny pie filled with chocolaty fudge.

Ingredients

1 stick butter, melted
¼ cup self-rising flour
¼ cup cocoa
2 eggs
1 teaspoon vanilla
1 cup sugar
1-2 refrigerated pie crusts, at room temperature

Directions

1. To make the pie filling, stir first six ingredients together with a fork until combined.

To make pie in mason jars

2. Grease six half-pint short jars with cooking spray.

3. Unroll one pie crust and use the mason jar lid as a template to cut six circles one inch wider than the lids. Press into mason jar and gently cover bottom and half way up sides.

4. Add three heaping tablespoons pie filling to mason jars and spread with back of spoon.

5. Wipe the jar rims and place in oven at 300 degrees for forty minutes. Let cool five minutes and add a scoop of vanilla ice cream to the top.

TO MAKE MINI FUDGE PIES IN MASON JAR LIDS

(The measurements for this recipe are for regular lids but wide mouth lids work too and produce bigger pies.)

1. Grab a mason jar lid and put the disk and ring together. This recipe makes about sixteen pies so you will need that many lids. Turn upside down and grease with cooking spray.

2. Unroll two pie crusts and use the mason jar lid as a template to cut sixteen circles one centimeter wider than the lids. Press into lid and gently cover bottom and sides. Use a fork to prick the dough a few times.

3. Add one tablespoon chocolate pie filling and spread with back of spoon.

4. Place pies on a pan and bake at 300 degrees for forty minutes. Let cool.

S'MORES TRAIL MIX

As much as Little Miss Mason Jar loves ooey-gooey s'mores, the sticky mess is maddening. This snack is a good alternative and there is no need to chase children around the backyard with wet wipes for their filthy fingers.

Say goodbye to summer boredom by pitching a tent in the living room, find a flashlight and tell scary stories while munching on this mason jar treat with your little campers!

Ingredients

4 cups Golden Graham Cereal
2 cups mini marshmallows
2 cups chocolate chip morsels

Directions

Mix all ingredients together in a large bowl and fill half-pint mason jars.

PERFECT PRETZEL BITES

This bite size sweet and salty snack is perfect for almost any occasion. It makes a great hostess gift and can be prepared throughout the year to match any holiday or celebration. Simply sort through a bag of M&M candies to find the colors you need to coordinate with your functions and festivities or purchase the special seasonal candies to get the correct colors. Place these perfect pretzel bites into pint size mason jars and prepare to make somebody smile!

Ingredients

Square shaped pretzels (approximately seventy-five will fit on a cookie sheet)
Chocolate candy kisses
M&M candies

Directions

1. Place pretzels in rows on a cookie sheet, fitting as many as possible.

2. Unwrap chocolate kisses and place one on each pretzel.

3. Cook in the oven at 175 degrees for five minutes or until chocolate kisses are soft and slightly melted.

4. Place an M&M candy on top of each chocolate kiss.

5. Cool completely for six or more hours until set.

CARAMEL PECAN PRETZEL BITES

These snacks follow the same cooking method as the Perfect Pretzel Bites, but the pretzels are covered with Rolos chocolate caramel candies and pecans are perched on top. Mason Jars packed with these Caramel Pecan Pretzel Bites will spread southern comfort to friends and family in your neck of the woods in no time.

Ingredients

Square shaped pretzels or mini pretzels (approximately seventy-five will fit on a cookie sheet)
Rolos candy
Pecan halves

Directions

1. Place pretzels on a cookie sheet.
2. Unwrap Rolos candy and place one on each pretzel.
3. Cook at 350 degrees for three to five minutes or until candy is soft and just starting to melt.
4. Remove from oven and place a pecan on top.
5. Cool completely for six or more hours to set.

PEANUT BUTTER BANANA PUDDING

Sink your sweet tooth into some creamy Peanut Butter Banana Pudding layered with crushed Nutter Butter cookies and soft slices of bananas. This recipe makes Little Miss Mason Jar 'all shook up' with excitement. No Elvis tunes necessary!

If you need a quick, easy and delicious dessert, this is it. Perfect for making ahead and delightful when presented with a spoon tied around the jar with twine.

This recipe yields six half-pint mason jars.

Ingredients

1 3.4-ounce box instant banana crème pudding
2 cups milk
1 8-ounce tub Cool Whip, thawed
$1/3$ cup creamy peanut butter
2 large bananas, sliced
1 cup coarsely crushed Nutter Butter cookies

Directions

1. Using a whisk, mix pudding and milk for five minutes, until thick.

2. In a separate bowl, stir peanut butter into Cool Whip until combined. Add peanut butter mixture to pudding and whisk well.

3. Use an ice cream scoop to add ¼ cup pudding mixture to a half-pint mason jar. Add three banana slices on top of pudding and sprinkle with one heaping teaspoon cookie crumbs. Repeat two more times for a total of three layers ending with cookie crumbs on top.

4. Seal and refrigerate three hours or longer before serving.

CHOCOLATE MOLTEN MASON JAR CAKE

There is a lot to love about this mason jar sweet treat. Little Miss Mason Jar cannot decide what she likes best about this Chocolate Molten Mason Jar Cake recipe- its ooey-gooey chocolate center, the simple steps it takes to make it or the fact that it can be made ahead of time, making life a lot easier. All of the above sounds like a good answer to me.

Make these chocolate molten mason jar cakes a few days in advance and let sit at room temperature for thirty minutes before baking to avoid an extreme temperature change reaction (and a very messy oven).

Yields seven half-pint mason jars

Ingredients

12 ounces semisweet chocolate morsels
1¾ cups butter
½ cup heavy cream, room temperature
5 eggs
1 teaspoon salt
1 teaspoon vanilla
¾ cup sugar
⅔ cup flour

Cooking spray
3 tablespoons cocoa powder

Directions

1. Grease mason jars with cooking spray and sprinkle cocoa powder inside of the mason jar to coat bottom and sides.

2. In a microwave safe bowl, melt chocolate chips and butter together for two and a half minutes, stopping every thirty seconds to stir. When chocolate cools down a bit stir in heavy cream.

3. Add eggs, salt, vanilla, sugar and flour. Stir until combined.

4. Fill half-pint mason jars three-quarters of the way full. Refrigerate for one hour or up to four days. Bake at 400 degrees for ten to fifteen minutes, until edges are firm and the middle is still runny. Do not overcook.

5. Let cool five minutes before serving warm with whipped cream and a dusting of cocoa powder.

MASON JAR BARS

You don't need a photo I.D. to get into this bar and the only reason you will be stumbling home is because your belly will be full of delicious mason jar meals. Little Miss Mason Jar's bars consist of creative spreads of scrumptious food and beverages set up and served buffet style.

Building a mason jar bar is a wonderful way to add some style to your next celebration. Setting up a delightful display of mason jars filled with festive foods gives gatherings a fun feeling and is a unique way for guests to serve themselves.

Stock the bar with more mason jars to use in place of bowls to enhance the charm.

MASON JAR CUPCAKE BAR

Set up a mason jar cupcake bar and allow your guests to create their own cupcakes by using assorted flavors and colors of cupcakes and frosting choices. Cut cupcakes in half, horizontally for layering. Offer toppings like sprinkles, M&M candies, chopped peanut butter cups, shredded coconut, crumbled cookies or mini chocolate chips.

ICE CREAM SUNDAE MASON JAR BAR

When the sweltering hot days of summer appear, it is best to have some ice cream near! Setting up an ice cream sundae mason jar bar is a fun activity for a child's birthday party or ice cream social and brings out the kid in us all.

Fill mason jars with tempting toppings to create a pretty presentation. Scoop ice cream in half-pint mason jars and let guests select their sweet treats to go on top. A well-stocked ice cream sundae bar should have assorted candy bars chopped into small pieces, fresh fruit, chocolate sauce, caramel sauce, nuts, rainbow sprinkles, chocolate sprinkles, mini marshmallows, gummy bears, M&M candies, crushed cookies, whipped cream, and maraschino cherries, of course.

MASON JAR YOGURT BAR

Yummy yogurt is layered with fruit and granola with this nutritious mason jar bar. Set up a simple selection of yogurt, fresh and dried fruit and crunchy granola. Personal yogurt parfaits are made in half-pint mason jars and eaten right away or fill your fridge for a quick breakfast on a manic morning.

MASON JAR CHILI BAR

Looking for a fun way to cheer up a chili loving crowd during tailgates or a backyard bonfire bash? Try setting up a mason jar chili bar for your guests to make their own chili creations.

Make a batch of chili without the cornbread topping (page 78) and keep it warm in a crock pot. Fill mason jars with chili and tasty toppings like sliced jalapenos, a variety of shredded cheeses (sharp cheddar, Monterey Jack, pepper jack), diced onions, sour cream, sliced green onions, mini cornbread muffins (for crumbling), Fritos, saltine crackers (bites size oyster crackers would be perfect)and tortilla chips.

Give your guests a pint size mason jar to hold their chili station creations!

MASON JAR BLOODY MARY BAR

Each summer when we take our fun-filled family vacation to the forgotten coast for seven days full of sun, surf and sand, my sister-in-law takes charge of our Bloody Mary bar. She builds the bar with traditional Bloody Mary garnishes then goes wild with unusual ingredients and creative concoctions. And when Little Miss Mason Jar says creative, she means it. Pickled brussel sprouts and green olives stuffed with Slim Jims, just to name a few. By the time I am done making my Bloody Mary I find myself needing a fork to help locate all of the little treasures that have sunk to the bottom. It's like a salad in a cup with a cocktail as a dressing.

Set up your mason jar Bloody Mary bar by using half-pint mason jars to hold the garnishes. Pour your favorite Bloody Mary mix into pint size mason jars and guests can gather their favorite garnishes. Impress your guests with dill pickle spears, cocktail onions, marinated mushrooms, romaine lettuce leaves, whole pickled okra, celery stalks, marinated asparagus spears, olives, capers, cucumber spears, stuffed olives with bleu cheese, garlic cloves, or Slim Jims, cooked bacon slices and pickled green beans.

MASON JAR ANTIPASTO BAR

Whether you are hosting an Italian theme dinner party or just looking for an appetizer to enjoy with a nice glass of wine and a loaf of bread, a mason jar antipasto bar is just what you need. Fill pint and quart size mason jars with Italian inspired foods like olives, salami cubes, grape tomatoes, marinated artichoke hearts, pepperoni, mozzarella and provolone cheese cubes, roasted garlic, peppers, marinated mushrooms and marinated onions. Everyone will find their favorite Ingredients and have their own tour of Italy tucked away in a half-pint mason jar.

MASON JAR CEREAL BAR

A mason jar cereal bar may seem a bit boring but trust Little Miss Mason Jar, it has its calling in the kitchen. Hosting a sleepover anytime soon? Set up a mason jar cereal bar and let the little ones wake up to a super cereal surprise. If children will be attending a brunch you are hosting, have a special kids table dedicated to a mason jar cereal bar just for them.

Have half-pint or pint size mason jars filled three-quarters of the way with a few varieties of cereal. Flaunt fresh fruits such as sliced strawberries, sliced bananas, blueberries and raspberries from pint size mason jars. Finish with cold milk in drink dispensers and scatter some spoons around. It's a morning made easy with a mason jar cereal bar!

MASON JAR SALAD BAR

Take your salad from plain to pleasant by preparing a mason jar salad bar. Add one cup of lettuce or spinach to pint size mason jars and indulge in all of the traditional toppings served on a salad bar. Pack pint and quart size mason jars with colorful veggies, cheeses, olives, croutons, grilled chicken or crumbled bacon. Add salad dressing and shake with the lid on before eating.

MASON JAR SNACK BAR

A mason jar snack bar is basic but convenient when kids come around. Hungry bellies will be happy to select snacks spilling out of large mason jars, into their fickle little fingers. Choose snacks kids love to chomp on like goldfish, pretzel sticks, mini marshmallows, raisins, dried banana slices, peanuts (check for allergies first), Cheerios or Chex cereal, popcorn, crackers, Teddy Grahams, or cheese puffs. Kids will love making their own mason jar meal for their next snack attack. To help them keep track of their snack, have them write their name on a chalkboard painted mason jar lid (page13).

MASON JAR MIMOSA BAR

Make your next bridal shower or brunch memorable with a mason jar mimosa bar. Invite your guests to make mimosas in mason jars by mixing fancy fruit juices with sparkling champagne. Try something other than traditional orange juice such as pomegranate juice, cranberry juice, apple juice, and grapefruit juice or mix a few fruit juices together. Sliced strawberries, orange wedges and maraschino cherries are great garnishes.

Author Biography

Randi Shiver (also known as Little Miss Mason Jar) is a wife and the mother of two busy boys. She teaches kindergarten and spends her free time cooking and crafting while documenting each detail along the way. Her recipes and food articles have been published in local magazines and newspapers in Florida's capital where she was born and raised.